1 2 3 4 5 6 7 8 9 10 20 30

FROM ONE
TO
ONE HUNDRED

Teri Sloat

40 50 60 70 80 90 100

Dutton Children's Books   New York

To Rebecca,
whom I can always count on

one

 two

2

three

four

4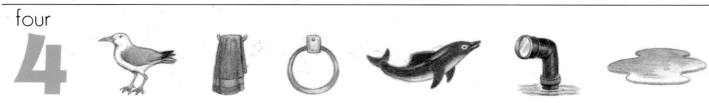

7

nine

9

ten

 10

twenty

20

thirty

30

forty

40

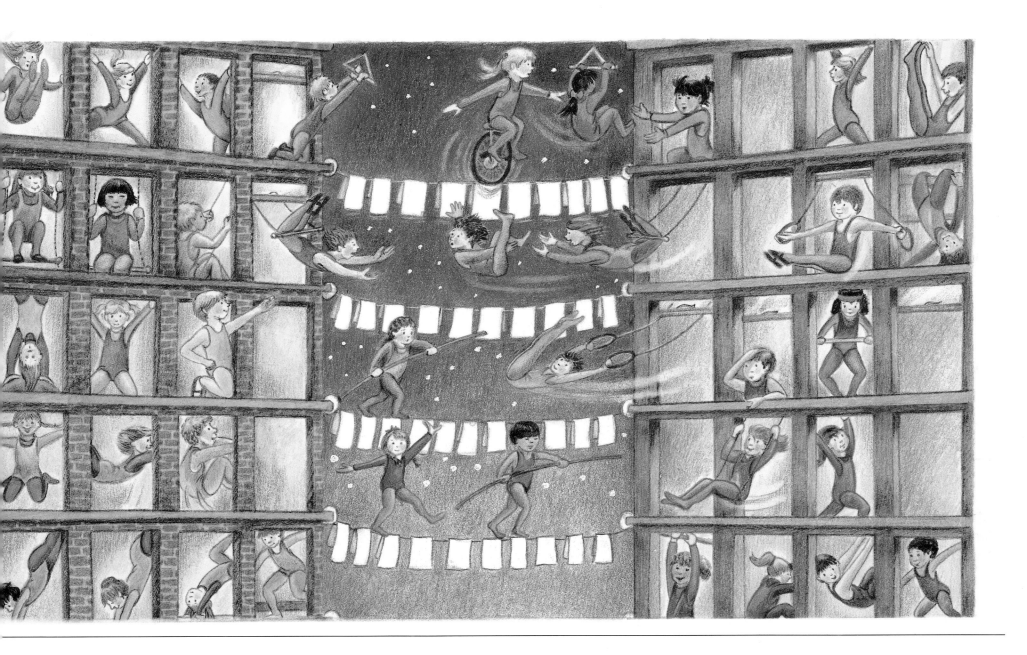

fifty
50

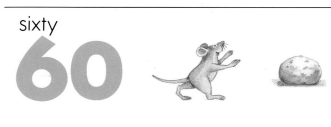

eighty

80

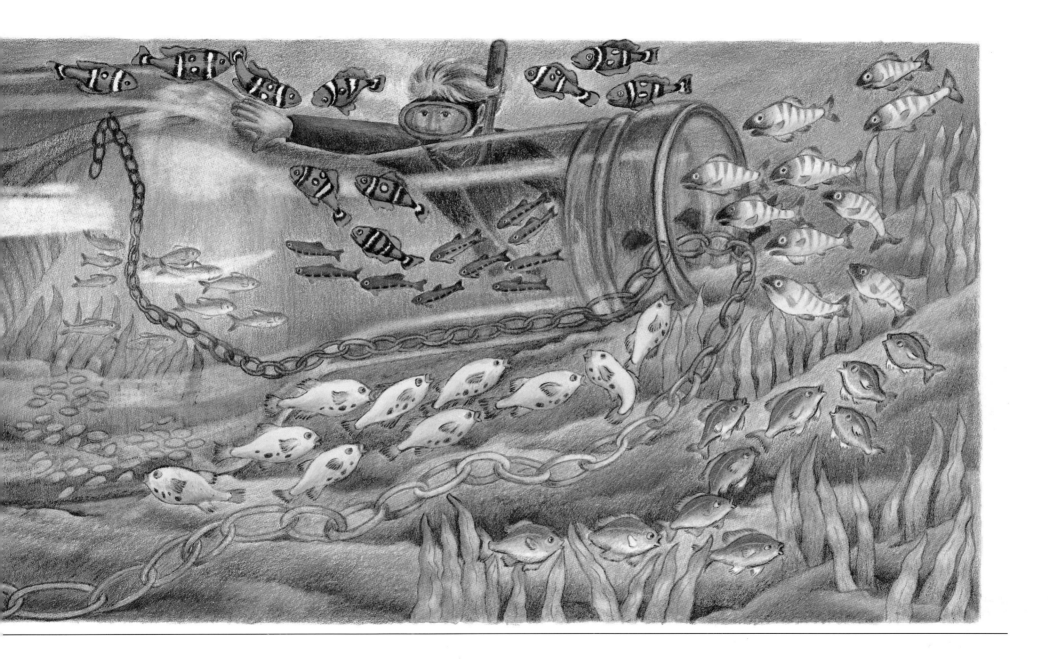

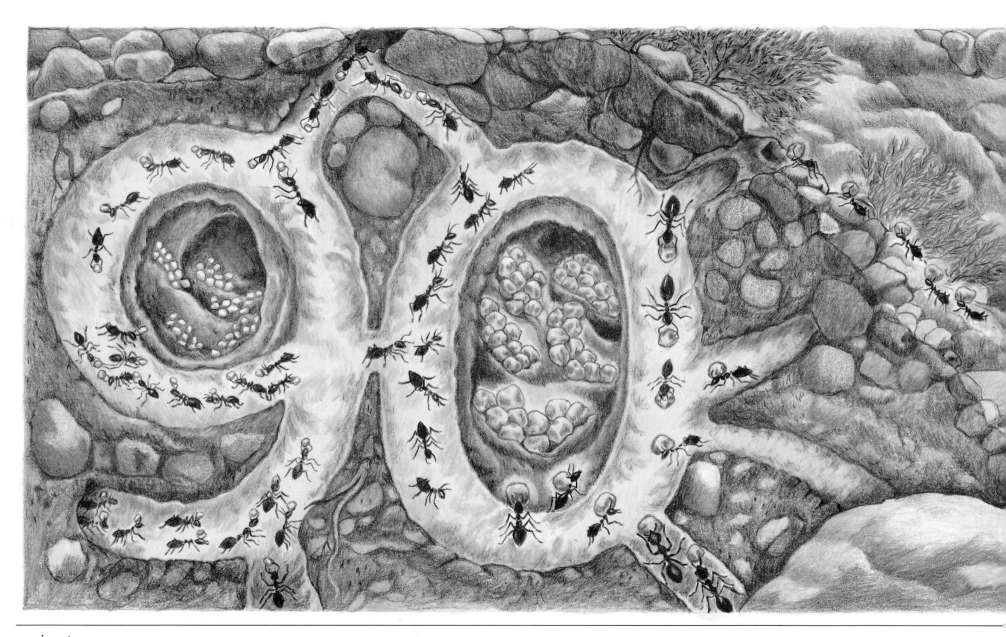

one hundred

100

1 2 3 4 5 6 7 8 9 10 20 30

Copyright © 1991 by Teri Sloat
Library of Congress Cataloging-in-Publication Data
Sloat, Teri.
From one to one hundred / Teri Sloat.—1st ed.
p.   cm.
Summary: Illustrations of people and animals introduce the numbers
one through ten and then, counting by tens, continue to one hundred.
ISBN 0-525-44764-4
1. Counting—Juvenile literature.   [1. Counting.]   I. Title.
QA113.S57   1991
513.2'11—dc20   91-21948   CIP   AC

Published in the United States by Dutton Children's Books,
a division of Penguin Books USA Inc.
375 Hudson Street, New York, N.Y. 10014

Designer: Riki Levinson

Printed in Hong Kong by South China Printing Co.
First Edition   10 9 8 7 6 5 4 3

40 50 60 70 80 90 100